Energy from Plants

by James Anderson

PEARSON
Scott Foresman

DK

What are plants' characteristics?

Plant Cells

How are a giant redwood tree in California and a small dandelion alike? They are both living things. They both have many cells. They are both in the plant kingdom.

The redwood tree and the dandelion are also different. The redwood tree grows about 90 meters tall. The dandelion comes a little above your ankle.

Look at a piece of a redwood tree and a piece of a dandelion under a microscope. They have similar parts that are similar sizes. These parts are cells. Plants are made of cells. Plant cells are grouped into tissues. Tissues that work together form organs.

Plants have many parts. Some parts take in water and materials from soil. Other parts use energy from the Sun to turn water and materials into food. Other parts move food to cells throughout the plant.

How Plants Make Food

Plants need sunlight and water to live, grow, and reproduce. They need carbon dioxide from the air. They also need mineral nutrients from the soil.

Photosynthesis

Plants make their own food. The food is sugar. **Photosynthesis** is the process of making this sugar. For photosynthesis, plants need carbon dioxide from the air. They need water from the soil.

There are tubes in the stem of the plant. Water and nutrients move through the tubes from the roots to the leaves. Plants use energy from the Sun to change these materials into food.

Tubes in the stem carry water and sugar.

Water travels through the plant's tubes to its leaves. In the leaves, tubes called veins carry water to the cells.

The thick outer layer of the stem protects the plant cells.

Oxygen and sugar are left when photosynthesis is complete. Oxygen moves out of plant leaves through tiny holes in the bottom of the leaves.

The tubes also move sugar to parts of the plant that need food. Roots, stems, and leaves store extra sugar.

Chloroplasts

Photosynthesis happens in the chloroplasts of the cells in leaves. Chloroplasts have **chlorophyll.** This makes them green. Chlorophyll takes in energy from the Sun. Plants use this energy to turn water and carbon dioxide into sugar and oxygen.

Cross Section of a Leaf

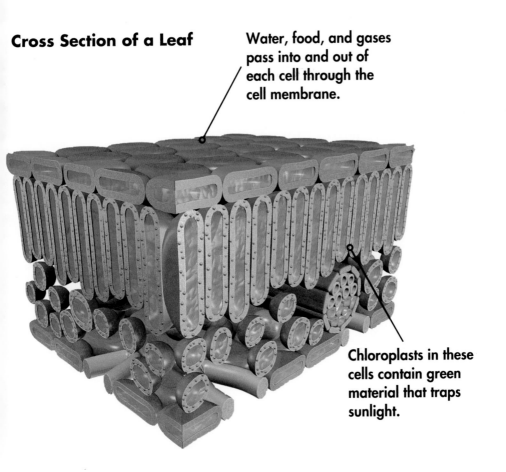

Water, food, and gases pass into and out of each cell through the cell membrane.

Chloroplasts in these cells contain green material that traps sunlight.

What are the parts of plants?

The Roles of Leaves and Stems

Groups of cells do certain jobs. Some cells make food. Some carry nutrients through the plant. Cells that do the same job make tissues. Wood is a tissue. Tissues work together to make organs. Roots, stems, and leaves are all organs. Most plants including the redwood tree and the dandelion have these parts.

Leaves

Leaves make food for a plant. Leaves can be different shapes and sizes. The different sizes and shapes help plants live in different environments. A pine tree has thin, sharp needles. This keeps them from losing too much water. A banana plant can have leaves that are wider than a kitchen table!

Leaves may be different shapes and sizes. But they all produce food for the plant.

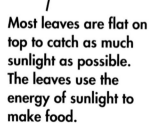

Most leaves are flat on top to catch as much sunlight as possible. The leaves use the energy of sunlight to make food.

Stems

A tree trunk is similar to the stalk of a grass plant. Both are stems. Stems have two important jobs. They move food, water, and minerals between the roots and the leaves. They also hold the plant up so its leaves can get sunlight.

A tree trunk is a hard stem. It grows thick and strong. It can support a large plant. Bark is made of a layer of dead cells. Bark protects the plant.

Some stems are soft. They bend easily. Daisies and dandelions have soft stems. These stems are often green. They carry out photosynthesis.

A waxy covering protects the stem. It prevents the stem from drying out.

The woody stems of trees and shrubs are hard.

The Roles of the Roots

Roots hold a plant in the ground. Roots take in mineral nutrients and water from the soil. Roots do not make food. They have no chlorophyll. Some roots can store food. This food is used when the plant cannot produce enough food through photosynthesis.

Fibrous Roots

Roots absorb water and nutrients. Roots grow away from the stem. The roots of some plants spread in many directions. They form a fibrous root system. These roots can take in water and mineral nutrients from a large area. Trees and most grasses have fibrous roots.

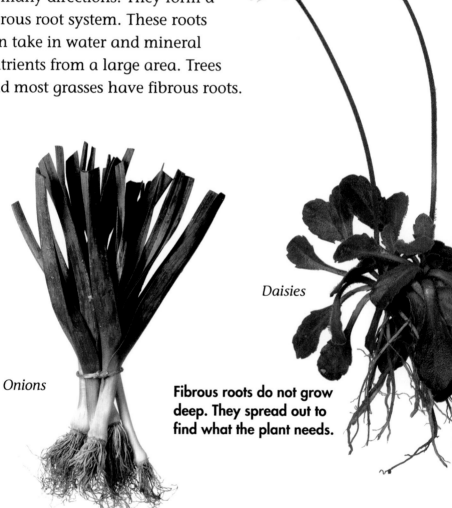

Daisies

Onions

Fibrous roots do not grow deep. They spread out to find what the plant needs.

8

Taproots

Plants such as dandelions, turnips, and carrots have a large main root called a taproot. A taproot grows straight down. It takes in water and nutrients from the soil. The root becomes thicker when it stores food. Smaller roots grow from the side of a taproot.

A root has tiny hairs sticking out around it. These root hairs allow the root to take in more mineral nutrients and water.

Tiny root hairs take in water and mineral nutrients.

Radish

Plants Without Roots

Some plants are able to get what they need without roots. They are called air plants. They take in moisture from the air. They take in nutrients from dust in the air. Spanish moss is an air plant.

9

How do plants reproduce?

Parts of Flowers

Scientists classify plants in many ways. One way is by how they make new plants, or reproduce. Plants that reproduce are put into two groups. Plants that make seeds are in one group. This group contains flowering plants and conifers.

Most flowers have four main parts. The easiest part to see is the petal. Petals can be colorful. They protect the seed-making parts. They attract living things such as bees, birds, and butterflies.

Pistil

Stamen

Petals

Small green leaves grow below the petals. Each leaf is called a **sepal.** The sepals cover and protect the flower bud. The sepals are pushed apart as the flower bud opens.

At the center of the flower are small, knoblike parts. These parts make up the **pistil.** The pistil is the female part of the plant. It makes egg cells.

Smaller stalks are around the pistil. Each stalk is a **stamen.** The stamens are the male parts of the plant. They have structures called anthers at their tips. Anthers make tiny grains of pollen. The sperm in the pollen combines with the egg cells in the pistil to make seeds.

Incomplete Flowers

Some flowers do not have the four main parts. The corn plant has two kinds of flowers. One is a male flower with stamens but no pistils. The other is a female flower that has pistils but no stamens.

Sepal

Pollen on the Move

A seed forms when pollen gets from a stamen to a pistil. Animals can help move pollen.

Nectar is a sweet liquid that flowers make. This is food for bees, birds, butterflies, and bats. They are drawn to the nectar by the scent of a flower and the color of its petals.

While the animal eats, pollen on the stamens rubs onto its body. That pollen may then rub onto the pistil of the next flower the animal visits. So the pollen moves from one plant to another. This is called pollination.

When pollen lands on a pistil, a thin tube grows from the pollen down to the thick bottom part of the pistil. This bottom part is called the **ovary.** Egg cells are in the ovary. The sperm cells in the pollen move down the pollen tube into the ovary. A sperm cell and an egg cell come together. This is **fertilization.**

Fertilization

A flower changes after fertilization. The petals and stamens dry up and fall off. The plant does not need them. Inside the ovary, the fertilized egg becomes a seed. The ovary gets bigger. It may become a fruit. This fruit protects the seed or seeds. Some fruits are moist and fleshy, such as apples or grapes. Some are dry and hard, such as a peanut shell. When the fruit is ripe, the seeds can form new plants.

One ragweed plant can release millions of grains of pollen into the air.

The wind pollinates grasses and most trees. The wind moves the pollen from stamens to pistils. Plants that use wind for pollination do not attract animals. They do not have bright colors or sweet scents. They make a lot of pollen for the wind to carry. This way, at least a few grains of pollen will land on another flower.

What is the life cycle of a plant?

Life Cycle of a Flowering Plant

Different plants live for different periods of time. A tomato plant may only live for a few months. A bristlecone pine tree can live for more than 4,000 years! A plant's life cycle includes every change a plant goes through during its life.

Seed coat

Leaf

Stem

Root

When a seed begins to grow, or germinate, it takes in water. It swells. The seed coat opens.

The young plant inside the seed uses stored food to grow. The first root and the first stem push through the seed coat.

The leaves grow. They make food for the plant through photosynthesis. The stem and roots grow. More leaves form.

The seedling grows into an adult plant. The plant inherits the color of the flowers from its parents.

The plant might flower and make seeds for many years. Eventually, the plant will die. Its life cycle will be complete.

When a flower is pollinated it produces fertilized eggs. These eggs develop into seeds. The new seeds germinate. The cycle begins again.

A seed may not grow as soon as it falls to the ground. A seed will only sprout when its environment is the right temperature. The seed also needs the right amount of oxygen and water in order to start to grow. If it does grow, the roots will grow into the ground. This is because of gravity. The new stem will grow upward. It grows toward the sunlight.

Seeds on the Move

Suppose all the cherries on a cherry tree fell to the ground. Many of the seeds would start to grow. Some seeds would grow better if they were farther away from the parent tree. Then they could get more water, nutrients, and sunlight. Many plants have adaptations that allow their seeds to be moved.

Animal Helpers

Some animals eat fruits with seeds. The seeds in the animals' droppings are then left at new places. Some fruits have tiny hooks that attach to animals' fur. The fruits fall off the animals. The seeds are moved to new places. Some animals bury seeds and nuts for the winter. These seeds and nuts may grow where they are buried.

Wind as a Helper

Dandelion puffs are made of small white threads. These threads catch in the wind and fly far away. Cottonweed puffs and milkweed plants also have these threads.

Maple trees have wing-shaped fruits. They twirl through the air. Tumbleweeds blow across the land in the southwestern part of the United States. Seeds fall off the plant.

Water as a Helper

Some seeds are carried by water. Coconuts are the fruits of one kind of palm tree. They can float on water to new places. There the seed may become a tree.

Seeds can move in many ways. Yet most seeds do not grow into new plants.

Animals can help move seeds from one place to another.

Starting to Grow

A seed may not grow as soon as it falls to the ground. The environment must be right for the seed to grow. A seed needs water, oxygen, and the right temperature.

A seed holds a young plant. Food in the seed gives the plant the energy it needs to begin growing. If a seed does not have everything it needs, it rests, or stays **dormant,** and does not grow. It can stay dormant for a long time.

Spores

Some plants do not grow from seeds. They grow from spores. A spore is made of only one cell. You can only see it with a microscope. It stores very little food. A spore must have the right environment to grow. A spore needs wet ground and constant moisture. Then it can become a new plant.

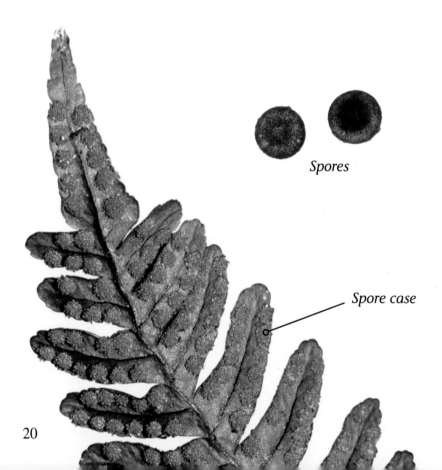

Spores

Spore case

A Two-Step Cycle

Some plants with spores reproduce in two steps. First, the plant produces a spore. The spore can germinate. It grows into a plant with both male and female cells. The male and female cell combine. This is the second step. This produces a fertilized egg that grows into a plant.

Spore cases hold spores. These cases can burst. This releases many spores into the air. The spores may land near the parent plant. They may drift far away. The spores will stay dormant until the conditions are right. Then the spores can begin to grow into new plants.

Spores go in every direction when spore cases burst.

New Plants From Plant Parts

Some plants grow from leaves, roots, or stems. These plants are usually just like the parent plant.

A tulip can start from a bulb. A bulb is an underground stem. It is made of thick layers of leaves that store food. The leaves grow up out of the soil. They turn green and make food.

Smaller plants can grow right on the leaves of a parent plant. The piggyback plant is one such plant. Potato sprouts grow from its buds or eyes. These sprouts can become new potato plants.

New Plants from Stems

Some plants have stems called runners. Runners grow along the ground. Roots grow from some spots on the runners, and leaves develop. New plants will grow from these leaves and roots. Strawberries have runners.

Amaryllis

Crown Imperial lily

Strawberry

Grafting

An apple grower may have an apple tree that grows good apples but has weak roots. Another apple tree may have strong roots but bad apples. The apple grower can join together branches from each tree. This is called grafting. Grafting will work only if the tubes that carry food, water, and nutrients in the plant match up. Then new tubes will grow.

Plants have many different parts that work together as a system. Throughout their lives, they are always growing and changing.

Potato plant

Hyacinth

Glossary

chlorophyll   the material that makes plants green and uses energy from the Sun to make food

dormant   in a state of rest

fertilization   the process in which a sperm cell and an egg cell come together

ovary   the part of the pistil of a plant that produces egg cells

photosynthesis   the process in which plants use sunlight, carbon dioxide, and water to make food for themselves

pistil   the female part of the plant

sepal   a small green leaf below the petals that covers and protects a flower

stamen   the male part of a plant that produces pollen